Published by SimpleTruths, LLC
1952 McDowell Road, Suite 300
Naperville, Illinois 60563
800-900-3427
www.simpletruths.com

Design and production: Scott Francis

Printed and bound in the United States of America

WOZ 10 9 8 7 6 5 4 3 2

SECRETS of the
World Class

Turning Mediocrity into Greatness

steve siebold

Table of Contents

World-Class Wealth Begins With World-Class Thinking 1

Champions Have An Immense Capacity For Sustained Concentration 5

Champions Are Driven By Emotional Motivators 9

The Great Ones Separate Truth From Fact 13

Champions Lead through Facilitated Introspection 17

The Great Ones Know They Are Unaware 21

Champions Develop World Class Beliefs Long Before They Become Champions 25

Professional Performers Don't Require Immediate Compensation 29

The World Class Operates From Objective Reality 33

Champions Know Adversity Is The Catalyst Of Mental Toughness 37

Middle Class Vs. World Class 41

The Great Ones Choose Discipline Over Pleasure 45

Champions Are Decisive 49

Common Sense Is The Foundation Of High Performance............................... 53

Champions Evolve From Competing To Creating........................... 57

Champions Understand Logic vs Emotion.................................... 61

The Great Ones Believe They Cannot Fail ... They Can Only Learn & Grow........... 65

The Great Ones Don't Give Back ... They Just Give 69

The World Class Has Great Expectations 73

Champions Are Driven By A World-Class Belief System......................... 77

Champions Take Risks 81

The Great Ones Take Responsibility 85

Champions Thrive On World Class Self-Talk 89

The Great Ones Make The Complicated Simple.............................. 93

The Great Ones Have A Sense Of Urgency 97

The Great Ones Are Learning Machines 101

The Great Ones Use Mentors 106

INTRODUCTION

I have had the privilege of competing against, coaching, being coached by and observing world-class performers since I was six years old. As a junior tennis player competing throughout the United States from ages 7 – 18, I became fascinated with what it takes to become a champion. My dream was to be ranked among the Top 10 players in the world, but I fell short. At my best, I hovered around the Top 500 in the world, and that's as high as I could seem to reach. Deep down, I knew I had the talent to make my dream a reality, and I knew the missing link was mental. After I hung up my racquet for the last time, I became obsessed with uncovering the mental toughness secrets of champions.

Starting in 1984, I spent every free moment conducting interviews with champions, reading their books and studying everything I could get my hands on about the psychology of peak performance. My friends said I was obsessed. They were right. This book is the result of my 20-year obsession.

When I started to implement the ideas in this book, my whole life changed. It wasn't overnight, but sometimes it seemed like it. There's

no magic here, just practical thought processes, habits and philosophies drawn from the greatest performers in the world.

This book contains no theories. Every secret comes straight from the street of experience, either my own or that of our clients. This book is loaded with ideas you can implement immediately. Some will be familiar and some new. All of them have the power to catapult your results, no matter how high you're flying. It's been said that speakers and writers espouse wisdom on the very topic they need most. Now that you know my story, you know this is true for me. After 20 years of studying and teaching mental toughness to people throughout the United States, Canada and 10 other countries, I can honestly tell you that many times I still think like a complete amateur, operating out of the same middle-class consciousness that I ridicule in this book. After all these years, my mental toughness growth is still a work in progress. The good news is that mental toughness is a skill that can be learned, and the tougher you get, the bigger you'll dream and the more fun you'll have.

~ Steve Siebold

SECRETS 1

World-Class
Wealth
Begins with World-Class
Thinking

$\mathcal{I}$f you got out of bed this morning and went to work because you wanted to, you are in control of money. If you got out of bed this morning because you had to, money is in control of you. Even in the wealthiest nation in the world, 99% of the population is being controlled by money. The effect is lack of money. The cause is thinking.

Albert Einstein once said, "A problem cannot be solved at the level of consciousness in which it occurs." Knowing this, champions raise their level of consciousness by studying how the world class creates wealth. The middle class believes formal education is the answer to acquiring wealth, yet very few academics are wealthy. They seek advanced degrees and certifications and are confounded when these things don't bring them riches. While the great ones are strong advocates of higher education, they don't believe it has much to do with acquiring money.

The middle class trades time for money. The world class trades ideas that solve problems for money.

"**Wealth** is the product of a man's **capacity** to **think.**"

~Ayn Rand
Author, Philosopher
1905-1982

Money flows like water from ideas. The middle class often scorns the world class out of frustration over a lack of money, yet the answer to earning more than they can spend has been in their laps their whole lives. Ideas – it's such a simple concept that the majority misses it. The poverty class talks about and regurgitates the past; the middle class talks about other people; and the world class talks about ideas. Professional performers know money doesn't care which direction it flows. They know the world will bend over backward to make them rich if it will help them solve their problems.

About 150 years ago, Karl Marx was sure the working class, as a whole, would rise up and overcome oppression if they had a chance. What Marx didn't figure into the equation was the poverty-driven thought process of the people. Give people operating at middle-class consciousness a million-dollar opportunity, and they will find a way to make it back to the middle class. It is where their limited self-image tells them they belong. The difference has nothing to do with reality. It's all perception in the mind of the performer.

ACTION STEP FOR TODAY

Ask this Critical Thinking Question:

"At what level of monetary success do I feel most comfortable?"

a. Poverty Class   **b.** Middle Class   **c.** World Class

Where you feel most comfortable reflects your self-image, and most likely, your current status. If you want to become wealthier, begin by raising your self-image by upgrading the self-talk you use regarding money and finances. If all you do is chase more money, you are simply attacking the effect.

The cause is how you think,
and if you improve the cause, *the effect will take care of itself.*

CHAMPIONS

Have an IMMENSE CAPACITY for

Sustained

CONCENTRATION

Champions are famous for concentrating their energy and efforts on what they want and blocking out anything or anyone who threatens that focus. While average people haphazardly pursue loosely defined goals, champions concentrate on the attainment of a singular purpose with an intensity that borders on obsession.

World-class performers invest an inordinate amount of time and energy in selecting their major goals. While the masses consider making changes every New Year's Eve, the goal setting and planning process is an everyday habit of champions. When the goals are set, champions put mental blinders on and move forward with dogged persistence and ferocious tenacity. World-class performers create such an intense level of concentration to overcome challenges and achieve goals that it is the last thing they think about before they fall asleep, and the first thing that hits them when they

"Nothing can add more POWER to your life than concentrating all your ENERGIES on a limited set of targets."

~Nido Qubein
Speaker, Author, Philanthropist

wake up. The great ones dream about their goals so frequently that they often keep pen and paper on the nightstand so they can quickly record any ideas or solutions that come to them in the middle of the night. While average people see world-class performers' successes as a matter of intelligence or luck, champions know sustained concentration of thought and action is usually the true key to their success.

ACTION STEP FOR TODAY

Write down the single most important goal you want to achieve in the next twelve months and make a commitment to concentrate on achieving it –

no matter what it takes.

"**Sustained concentration** is a learnable skill. It's not something you're born with; it's something you develop through **daily practice.**"

SECRETS 3

Champions
are driven by
EMOTIONAL MOTIVATORS

The masses are primarily motivated by extrinsic motivators, such as material possessions and money. The world class is motivated intrinsically by their dreams, desires and passions. External motivation is short lived, while internal motivation is nearly impossible to exhaust until the goal is achieved. The rah-rah, jump-up-and-down motivational pep talks are fun and temporarily motivating, yet lack the real fire emotional motivators generate.

World-class leaders know the secret to motivating themselves and others is discovering what they will fight for when the going gets tough. The great ones move from logic-based motivators to emotion-based motivators. They know the key to finding the true power of the individual lies in the deep recesses of the psyche. The process great leaders and coaches use is tedious, time consuming and simple: ask questions, and don't stop until you have landed on the emotional hot buttons.

World-class coaches keep digging until they hit the vein of gold – when the performer begins answering in terms of how they feel, as opposed to what they think. When they hit the vein of gold, they continue to probe until the performer reaches an emotional high point, known in performance circles as the white moment. The white moment is the strongest emotional driver of a performer. Coaches use emotional drivers to motivate and inspire performers to push far beyond their threshold of pain, to accomplish feats that, without this level of motivation, would be impossible.

"**When a PERFORMER** begins to experience PHYSICAL OR EMOTIONAL PAIN in the heat of the battle, the **brain,** whose primary role is **self-preservation,** asks the question: 'Why must I suffer?' The champion will answer the question with the vision they have carefully constructed, and they will CONTINUE TO FIGHT. Since the masses lack this mental clarity and have no reason to suffer, they quit as soon as the pain kicks in. **Developing a world-class vision is the SECRET to world-class motivation.**"

~Steve Siebold

ACTION STEP FOR TODAY

Ask these 5 Critical Thinking Questions:

1. What am I willing to fight for?

2. What values do I hold dearest to my heart?

3. What values would I be willing to die for?

4. If I could achieve a single thing, what would make all my hard work worth the struggle?

5. If I had thirty seconds left to live, what would I tell my children are the three most important things I learned about how to live a happy life?

Your answers will tell you a lot about what drives you emotionally.

SECRETS 4

The Great Ones

Separate

Truth from

FACT

While average performers tend to believe truth and fact are the same, the world class knows there is a difference. Champions use their critical thinking skills to make a clear distinction between truth and fact. Fact is reality. Truth is our perception of reality, and perceptions are subjective. One person perceives giving to charity as an expense, while another perceives it as an investment in someone else's life. The fact is that many people give to charity; whether it's an expense or an investment is a perception. Which line of thinking represents truth? Both. In the minds of individuals, perception equals truth. This subtle distinction allows the great ones to understand themselves and others at a higher level of awareness.

The masses tend to operate from truth, which is often a distorted version of facts. Champions make decisions based on facts, not feelings. The world class also uses this understanding of truth and fact in their mental programming. The great ones know the conscious mind functions most effectively on fact, while the subconscious can be programmed with truth. Since the subconscious is unable to make the distinction between fact and truth, champions program their

"We have to live today by what TRUTH we can get today and be ready tomorrow to call it FALSEHOOD."

~William James
1842-191, Author

14

subconscious minds to believe their visions, dreams and ideas are truths. Because the subconscious doesn't have the ability to reject an idea, it accepts it as truth and begins to create behaviors that are congruent with this new "truth." The conscious mind knows this "truth" is not fact, and tension begins to build between the conscious and subconscious, creating cognitive dissonance. As a result, the two go to work to create congruency. The great ones are not only aware of the difference between truth and fact, but they also know how to use them both to get what they want.

ACTION STEP FOR TODAY

Write down two things you know are fact & rethink each by asking:

"Is this really a fact, or a truth I've created from my own or others' perceptions?"

For example:

Is it a fact that the sky is blue?
Is it a fact that you are a nice person?
Is it a fact that the faithful will be rewarded in heaven?

You'll see how often we operate from truth, rather than fact.

"When an event occurs, the brain
asks itself three questions:

What is it?
What does it mean?
What do I do?

If you change the meaning of the event
you automatically change the way the brain responds.
MEANINGS are **TRUTHS** that can be altered.
This gives world class performers
ultimate control over their lives."

SECRETS 5

Champions
Lead through
facilitated
Introspection

All great leaders know that the most effective form of learning is self-discovery. World-class coaches and managers believe in facilitating the introspective process, which helps people rediscover what they already know. Instead of leadership through the outdated command-and-control, do-it-or-you're-fired model, progressive managers are constantly asking their employees questions and taking careful note of their answers. The great ones know that most people are unaware of what makes them tick in terms of their emotional motivators. The only way to help a person discover the hidden power locked up in their psyche is by asking probing questions.

"The GREAT managers and leaders of the future will know more about their people than ever before. They'll know their EMOTIONAL HOT BUTTONS as well as the essence that makes them tick. Through facilitated introspection these leaders will create a competitive immunity for their companies by reigniting the flame of loyalty that burns within their people."

Learning occurs at two levels during this introspective process.

The first level is when the person digging down inside himself becomes aware of the emotions driving his behavior, and the second is the manager's awareness as it relates to which buttons to push when it's time to motivate his charge to action. Amateur coaches and managers coach primarily through logic. Professional coaches and managers coach primarily through emotion. Since human beings are primarily emotional creatures, it's obvious which method has the most power.

Facilitating the introspective process in another person requires patience and time, and the great ones are willing to invest. The amateur wants instant results, but pros know this rarely occurs. The payoff for the pro comes not only in the form of increased productivity, but also in the connection created between manager and employee. Once an emotional creature is convinced that you care about what she thinks and how she feels, it sets the stage for emotional bonding to occur. Managers and leaders who lead this way lose very few of their people to rival companies because of this bond. In the age of the mind, facilitated introspection is the core process of leadership.

ACTION STEP FOR TODAY

Invest 20 minutes today leading someone
through the INTROSPECTIVE PROCESS.

Your first question should be:
"Tell me what you really want out of life more than anything else."
Your goal should be to make the person comfortable enough to answer you
in terms of how she feels, rather than how she thinks.

Once she begins to explain her FEELINGS,
follow up with these questions:

What exactly do you mean by that?

What does that look like?

Why do you feel that way?

Tell me more about that.

Why is that important to you?

What does having that mean to you?

SECRETS 6

the GREAT ONES
Know
they are
Unaware

Champions have come so far in raising their levels of awareness that they realize there is always a higher level. Average people have a world view that says being comfortable with who and where they are in life is the key to happiness. The great ones have a world view that says happiness is learning, growing and becoming.

> **"Everyone** is operating and **running their lives** at their current level of **conscious awareness."**
>
> ~Carlos Marin
> Speaker and Author

School is never out for champions. The more they learn, the more they realize how much they don't know. While average people seek mental comfort, the world class believes mental comfort is the death of growth. They live by this phrase: "You're either growing or dying; stagnation does not exist in the universe." Like the child who always asks "why," champions always ask questions of other top performers in an effort to get new takes on old ideas. Their ongoing mental growth reinforces their beliefs of other levels of conscious awareness that can make them more successful, more fulfilled and happier.

World-Class Resource

Get a copy of

The Handbook to Higher Consciousness

by Ken Keyes Jr.

This timeless classic will provoke you to think at a higher level.

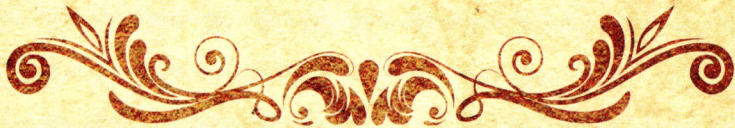

ACTION STEP FOR TODAY

Ask this Critical Thinking Question:

"Am I growing or dying?"

If your answer is dying, make the decision today to become
more aware and begin growing.

" The **ULTIMATE GOAL** of the world class thinker is to ascend to the highest level of **awareness** in the shortest amount of time.

The more aware you become, the more **successful, fulfilled** & **happy** you will be."

CHAMPIONS develop

World-Class
Beliefs

long before they become Champions

One of the major distinctions between average performers and champions is their belief system. Like champions, average people tend to be a product of their mental programming from childhood. People of influence, such as parents, teachers, coaches, religious leaders and others were the primary builders and shapers of our early belief systems. In most cases, this programming is limiting because it comes from people who believe they are limited. That's why average people are saddled with a set of beliefs that are more about survival than success. Average people have been programmed to avoid pain at all costs, which promotes a "playing not to lose" mentality.

Many world-class performers were raised with these same beliefs, yet learned to reprogram themselves somewhere along the way. Champions learn how to develop empowering beliefs and invest a substantial amount of time solidifying those beliefs, mostly through their own self-talk. With guidance from coaches and mentors, champions monitor the words they use. They know reprogramming is a never-ending activity. Some people even consider this process "positive brainwashing." When aspiring champions learn they can program any belief they wish, and through repetitious, ongoing self-talk, build that belief into a foundation for their consciousness, it's a revelation.

"They can...because they **think they can."**

~Unknown

A world-class belief system can be created from scratch, no matter what your age, upbringing or current lot in life. A world-class belief system is a primary factor in the making of a champion, and every great performer knows it. While average people see champions as more intelligent, the champions know better. The truth is that intelligence plays a small part. Belief is the real star of the show.

Action Step for Today

Make a list of your most closely held beliefs, and begin the process of questioning whether they are serving you or holding you back.

Question Their Validity

Are they relevant, or out of date?

Knowing that behavior follows belief, give yourself an opportunity to discard or upgrade any beliefs that limit you.

"World class thinking is a language made of beliefs and philosophies that serve your best interests and open the door to unlimited possibilities.

LEARN THE LANGUAGE and begin to speak it to yourself and others every day. In time,

you will begin to believe everything you're saying.

Your new behavior will be the product of your new beliefs."

Professional
PERFORMERS
Don't Require
immediate
compensation

$\mathcal{M}$ost people are fully engaged in microwave thinking - a deep belief that compensation should immediately follow any effort. Champions are different. They believe every effort performed with good intention yields some form of compensation at some point. People become champions by perfecting their competencies until other people label them "champion." In most cases, this label took years of hard work and sacrifice to achieve, with little or no apparent compensation along the way.

> ## "Did you think
> you could have the **good** without the evil?
> Did you think you could have the
> **joy** without the sorrow?"

Many of the great ones were ridiculed and criticized for investing so many hours in the development of their core competencies. Not swayed by amateur opinion, they pushed forward aggressively. This delayed gratification set the stage for all future battle plans for achievement in the minds of champions. When professional performers set a big goal, they are expecting a fight - and their past experience has preconditioned their minds for battle. When amateurs expect compensation, pros are just settling in for the fight. Their willingness to delay gratification and compensation makes them more valuable in the marketplace.

ACTION STEP FOR TODAY

Ask this Critical Thinking Question:

"Am I more interested in pleasure or gratification?"

Amateurs focus on pleasure-based activities that deliver short and sweet payoffs. Professionals focus on gratification-based activities that take longer to achieve but deliver long and deep payoffs.

Into which category do you fall?

"He who devotes sixteen hours a day to **hard study** may become at sixty as wise as he thought himself at twenty."

~ Mary Wilson Little

SECRETS 9

The World Class

OPERATES from

OBJECTIVE

REALITY

*I*n 20 years of competing, coaching and working with performers from various fields, I've discovered most amateurs suffer from mild to severe delusions in relation to their efforts and competencies. In other words, most people delude themselves into thinking they are working harder than they are, and that they are more competent than they actually are.

Of the five major levels of conscious awareness, (poverty, working, middle, upper and world) my experience has been that performers at the middle-class levels of consciousness suffer the grandest delusions. The poverty level is barely surviving and living in a very harsh set of circumstances. The working class is punching a mental time clock and counting the days until retirement.

"Amateur performers operate from delusion, **pros operate** from objective reality. The **GREAT ONES' HABITS, ACTIONS & BEHAVIORS** are totally congruent with the size & scope of their ultimate vision. **That's why we call them CHAMPIONS."**

They're usually not expecting much, and no one around them expects much either. They are typically not concerned about climbing any higher.

It's the middle class that is most incongruent with reality. They are operating at a high enough level to understand that higher levels exist. Although they don't expect to get there, the thought crosses their minds from time to time. Because of their low expectations, their actions are incongruent with their desires. In other words, they want to live the life of the world class, but are unwilling to pay the price. Since this reality is too harsh to bear, they delude themselves into thinking they are doing everything in their power to get ahead. Of course, they're not. They'll tell you they're putting in far more time than they are. They'll swear they are thinking about their vision all the time, but they're not.

The world class is brutally honest with themselves, and they tend to look reality in the face. They err on the side of over-practicing and over-preparing. Champions know that to ascend to the top, you must first be operating from a mindset of objective reality. Self-deception and delusion have no place in the professional performer's consciousness.

Action Step for Today

Make a commitment to check delusion at the door.

Be honest and ask this CRITICAL THINKING question:

"Are my habits, actions and behaviors congruent with the vision I have for my life?"

"Objective reality is in contrast to **subjective reality,** which is reality seen through our inner mental filters that are shaped by our past conditioning. OBJECTIVE REALITY is how things really are."

~ A.H. Almaas

CHAMPIONS know
ADVERSITY
is the Catalyst of
Mental
Toughness

$\mathcal{C}$hampions believe if you remove the adversity, you remove the victory. As a result, they tend to view adversity as a challenge through which learning and growing occurs. Their world view is evident in the way they describe the adversities they face. While average people choose the path of least resistance, world-class performers operate at a higher level of awareness. They understand that stress and struggle are the key factors in becoming mentally tough. While average people watch television and hang out at happy hour, the great ones continue to push themselves mentally and physically to the point of exhaustion. Only then will you see them in rest and recovery situations.

> **World-Class Resource**
>
> Read
> *Man's Search for Meaning*
> by Viktor Frankel
>
> It is the true story of how one man learned to control his thoughts, feelings and attitudes as a prisoner of war. It's a classic that should be a part of every champion's library.

"If it weren't for the dark days, we wouldn't know what it is to walk in the light."

~Earl Campbell
Professional Football player

Adversity, to average people, equals pain.

Adversity, to world-class performers, is their mental training ground. It's how they become mentally tough. Average people scorn adversity. Those who are world class don't welcome adversity; yet they see it as the ultimate catalyst for mental growth, as well as the contrast needed to recognize the beauty of life.

ACTION STEP FOR TODAY

List the three most difficult adversities you have faced and five good things that happened to you as a result of each one.

Train yourself to see the good in adversity, and your fear of future challenges will dissipate.

"You will never be the person you can be if **pressure, tension** & **discipline** are taken out of your life."

~James G. Bilkey

WORLD-CLASS

VS

MIDDLE-CLASS

The Middle Class competes… The World Class creates.

The Middle Class avoids risk… The World Class manages risk.

The Middle Class loves to be comfortable…
The World Class is comfortable being uncomfortable.

The Middle Class lives in delusion… The World Class lives in objective reality.

The Middle Class hungers for security…The World Class doesn't believe security exists.

The Middle Class sacrifices growth for safety…
The World Class sacrifices safety for growth.

The Middle Class focuses on having… The World Class focuses on being.

The Middle Class has a lottery mentality…
The World Class has an abundance mentality.

The Middle Class slows down … The World Class calms down.

The Middle Class is frustrated… The World Class is grateful.

The Middle Class operates out of fear and scarcity…
The World Class operates from love and abundance.

The Middle Class has pipedreams… The World Class has vision.

The Middle Class denies its intuition … The World Class embraces its intuition.

The Middle Class trades time for money…
The World Class trades ideas for money.

The Middle Class is problem oriented … The World Class is solution oriented.

The Middle Class sees itself as a victim…
The World Class sees itself as responsible.

The Middle Class thinks it knows enough… The World Class is eager to learn.

The Middle Class speaks the language of fear…
The World Class speaks the language of love.

The Middle Class chooses fear… The World Class chooses growth.

The Middle Class is boastful… The World Class is humble.

The Middle Class seeks riches … The World Class seeks wealth.

The Middle Class believes its vision only when it sees it …
The World Class knows it will see its vision when it believes it.

The Middle Class coaches through logic … The World Class coaches through emotion.

The Middle Class believes problem solving stems from knowledge …
The World Class believes problem solving stems from will

"Middle class consciousness is what most of us are born into.
World class consciousness is
what's possible."

SECRETS 11

The Great Ones Choose
Discipline
over Pleasure

hen average performers have had enough for the day and call it quits, champions are usually just getting started. Discipline is the watchword of great performers. Discipline makes the difference between the good and the great. The great ones will tell you discipline is more of a decision than it is an active skill. It's the ability to stay the course and complete promises you've made. The fulfillment of these promises builds confidence and self-esteem, which eventually leads champions to believe almost anything is possible. It's a habit and a self-fulfilling prophecy built into one. Discipline is a logic-based decision that performers adhere to, regardless of whether they feel like it or not.

"With self-discipline anything is possible. I believe discipline is the ultimate KEY TO SUCCESS as it determines your approach toward every day. Discipline keeps you focused & keeps you PERFORMING at a world-class level."

~Roger D. Graham Jr., Sr. Vice President, Marketing and Sales, Yamanouchi Pharma-America

Discipline pushes performers past pain and punishment. As my late business partner and mentor Bill Gove always said, "It's easier to act yourself into good thinking than it is to think yourself into good action." This is the mindset of the champion. The great ones, like Bill Gove, don't let feelings interfere with their performance. Instead, they harness the power of their emotional motivators to propel them past the competition. Average people see discipline as a painful chore to be avoided at all costs. The world class sees it as the ultimate power tool for performance.

ACTION STEP FOR TODAY

On a scale of 1 to 7, 7 being most disciplined,
how disciplined are you in the different areas of your life?

CATEGORIES INCLUDE:

BUSINESS / CAREER

FAMILY / FRIENDS

MONEY / FINANCES

RECREATION / FUN

HEALTH / DIET / EXERCISE

FAITH / SPIRITUAL

SOCIAL / CULTURAL

PERSONAL DEVELOPMENT

"Hold yourself responsible for a higher standard than anybody else expects of you. Never excuse yourself. Never pity yourself. **Be a hard master to yourself and be lenient to everybody else."** ~Henry Ward Beecher

SECRETS 12

Champions are Decisive

While average performers are timid and lack confidence in their own judgment, champions are known for their ability to make decisions, especially under pressure. The difference is courage and confidence. Even the best leaders are uncertain about their decisions in an environment of unprecedented change. The difference is their willingness to make a decision and take full responsibility for the outcome.

Amateur performers habitually play not to lose and procrastinate because they fear making a mistake. The great ones know mistakes will be made and can be corrected. Their willingness to assume full responsibility for their decisions eliminates the need to gather more input than is absolutely necessary. Developing a sound decision-making process, while understanding every decision is somewhat a gamble, is the foundation of superior leadership. Professional performers can lead people and organizations effectively under such high-pressure

> "If I had to sum up in one word **what makes a good manager**, I'd say DECISIVENESS. You can use the fanciest computers to gather the numbers, but in the end **you have to set a timetable & act.**"
>
> ~Lee Iacocca
> Former Chairman, Chrysler Corp.

World-Class Resource

Read
Grow Up!
by Dr. Frank Pittman

This book takes a no-holds-barred approach to taking personal responsibility.

constraints because they possess the self-trust necessary to make decisions without fear. Generally speaking, the higher the leadership position, the greater and the deeper the leader's self-trust must be. Courage, self-trust and the willingness to assume full responsibility for the outcomes of their decisions are mandatory traits of competent and effective leaders.

ACTION STEP FOR TODAY

Take a decision you have been putting off for a while and decide on a course of action within the next 24 hours.

Decision-making skills are like muscles:
they can only be built through use.

"A bad decision on Monday is better than a good one on Friday. What bedevils our business is **lack of speedy response.**"

~Sir Martin Sorrell

SECRETS 13

Common
SENSE
is the foundation of
HIGH Performance

Champions usually believe the essentials of life were learned in kindergarten. Their world view is that success is simple and constructed fundamentally from common sense. While average people search for complex answers to their problems, the world class looks for the simple solution first – and usually finds it. They solve more complex challenges by looking at situations as outsiders viewing them for the first time.

Larry Wilson, the famous speaker and author, says the great ones get out of their own way by viewing problems from ten thousand feet in order to gain a new perspective. They separate themselves from the everyday details and gain a three-dimensional view of problems.

> **"COMMON SENSE is the knack of SEEING THINGS AS THEY ARE, and doing things as they ought to be done."**
>
> ~Harriet Beecher Stowe, 1811-1896, Author of Uncle Tom's Cabin

While average people strain to create solutions, champions think for a while and then create a mental distance to take their direct focus off the problem. Many times the answers come to them in the shower, in the middle of the night, or at the health club while they're working out. The law of indirect effort is one of the most powerful problem-solving processes known to man. Champions realize the secret to tapping their true genius is sometimes hidden in the act of not trying so hard.

Action Step for Today

Write down your five most PRESSING PROBLEMS and ask:

*"Is there a kindergarten answer to this
seemingly complex problem?"*

Let your mind revert to childlike thinking
and write down the first answers that come to mind.

"**Common sense** in an uncommon degree is what the world calls wisdom."

~Samuel Taylor Coleridge

Champions Evolve from Competing to CREATING

*A*verage performers live their lives in first gear, resisting change and avoiding risk. The masses have the same talent and opportunity as the world class; yet choose to play it safe to avoid the pain of failure and the agony of (temporary) defeat.

At Mental Toughness University, we have a scale called The Five Levels of Mental Toughness, which is a tool to help people determine at what level they are performing. The first level is called Playing Not to Lose, which is doing just enough to avoid getting fired. The next level up is Playing to Cruise, which is mentally cruising through the job without really engaging in any serious thought. The next level is Playing to Improve, which is when performers begin to actively engage their thoughts and feelings in the tasks at hand, attempting to get better. The level above this is Playing to Compete, which is when performers begin to believe they are capable of beating out their competition and being the best.

"**Creative people** rarely need to be motivated – they have their own **INNER DRIVE** that refuses to be bored. They refuse to be complacent. **They live on the edge,** which is precisely what is needed to be successful and **remain successful."**

~Donald Trump
Real Estate Developer

This level is primarily ego-driven where winning is the main objective. Performers operating at this level often become very successful and powerful, but are sometimes left with hollow feelings of "Is this all there is?"

The highest level is Playing to Win, which occurs when the performer moves from competition to creation, where the primary goal is to be the best he or she can be. Knowing that creativity and fear cannot co-exist, these people are competing only with themselves with the objective of being better today than they were yesterday. The Playing to Win philosophy is rooted in a spirit-based consciousness operating from thoughts of love and abundance. Fear and scarcity have no place at this level of thinking. These performers are fearlessly seeking what Dr. Abraham Maslow referred to as Self-Actualization, or becoming all that one has the potential to become. The most powerful belief performers operating at this level possess is that they cannot fail; they can only learn and grow.

With their potential in front and their fear behind them, champions are able to move beyond the boundaries of competition and create what the masses believe is impossible.

Action Step for Today

Examine the 5 Levels of Mental Toughness and identify the level you inhabit most often in performance situations.

Make a commitment to spend as much time at the Playing to Win level as possible.

"Exchange is
creation"

~Muriel Rukeyser

Champions

Understand

Logic vs
Emotion

*A*mateur managers, coaches and leaders tend to favor either a logic-based approach to performance or an emotional-based approach. The pros know the magic is in the mix. When it comes to strategic planning and business acumen, straight logic is essential. Emotion creates confusion when it comes to linear thought. This is why amateurs in the business world have repeated the idea that there is no place for emotion in business. Professional leaders know this is ridiculous.

As you know, human beings are emotional creatures driven by emotional motivators like love, recognition, belonging, pride, values, etc. The list goes on and on. To ignore the role emotion plays in performance is to

"The arena was so loud, the emotion so great. Everybody was going crazy. I remember thinking, 'Stay with it. Don't get swept up. 'The **hotter** it gets the **cooler** you have to get. I remember thinking of one word in my mind – 'MIRACULOUS.' "

~Al Michaels
Sports Announcer, commenting on the 1980 U.S. Olympic Hockey Team victory over the Soviet Union

disregard the power of the fire that burns within a person's soul. The real distinction between amateur leaders and pros is that amateurs motivate through logic and the great ones motivate through emotion. Logic is great for planning, but weak for motivation. Trying to inspire an emotional creature by appealing to their sense of logic is amateur at best, and stupid at worst. In twenty years of studying and working with leaders, only a small percentage has really understood this in the business world.

In the world of professional sports, it's a different story. Many top coaches use emotional motivation brilliantly. The best example may be Herb Brooks, who motivated the U.S. Olympic Hockey team in 1980 to pull one of the greatest upsets in history. Emotional motivation has the power to drive a team beyond what they actually believe is possible. The sheer force of the collective emotion is so overwhelming that it mentally elevates the consciousness of the individual performers, which enables them to tap into a higher level of intelligence.

The secular philosophy is that the performers are able to access more of their brains when they are operating in this altered state of consciousness. The spiritual philosophy says that performers have raised their rates of vibration to the same frequency as the force that created the universe. While champions' belief in the source of this power varies, they all know that the process begins with emotional motivation.

"When we feel deeply,
we reason
profoundly."

~Mary Wollstonecraft

SECRETS 16

The Great Ones Believe THEY CANNOT FAIL...

They Can Only
LEARN &
GROW

Champions are committed to never-ending personal and professional growth. Average performers believe learning and growing begins and ends in school. The world-class ranks realize graduation is the beginning of the road, not the end. Professional performers attempt so many things over the course of their lifetimes that their mental growth rates are staggering compared to the masses. While amateurs avoid risk at any cost, the great ones are always looking for opportunities. They are willing to fail their way to success. The belief of the champion, according to author Larry Wilson is, "I cannot fail...I can only learn and grow."

This belief makes pros very dangerous performers. While average people attempt to win while simultaneously trying to avoid pain, champions give it the full-court press with little or no concern about failing. Champions have programmed themselves to disengage their fears and move full speed ahead. The middle and lower class are amateurs at failing; they are so afraid of it they only attempt goals they know they can reach. The feelings of bliss that champions experience don't stem from their successes, but from the fulfillment of the growth that occurred along the way.

"Growth itself contains the GERM OF HAPPINESS."

~Pearl S. Buck
1892-1973, Author

Action Step for Today

**Begin telling yourself YOU CANNOT FAIL;
you can only LEARN & GROW.**

Keep repeating these words to yourself at every opportunity
for the next 30 days, and see what happens.

You will create a new world-class belief that
may transform your life.

"If at first you don't succeed…
welcome to the club."

~Israel Harold Asper

SECRETS 17

The GREAT ONES DON'T GIVE BACK... They Just Give

World-class performers usually have a strong philosophy when it comes to giving. Middle-class consciousness is rooted deeply in fear, but world-class consciousness is rooted in love and abundance. Professional performers tend to have a world view that there is, and always will be, more than enough of everything to go around. As a result, they tend to give freely.

"Don't give back... just give."

~Nido Qubein
Author, Speaker, Philanthropist

People operating at poverty-, working-, and middle-class levels of awareness will give from time to time, yet there is a difference. They tend to give in order to get. In other words, people at lower levels of awareness often see giving as a trade, it's an "I give you this, so you have to give me that" mentality. The great ones give without reservation or anticipation of a trade. They give because they believe it's the right thing to do, and as a result, they experience much deeper levels of fulfillment than average people.

World-class performers are not more generous; they simply believe they'll never run out of resources and that the world operates from total abundance. Giving is easy when you believe the source of supply is unlimited. The world-class mindset is pure love, with no beginning, no end and no limits. The amateur-class philosophy demands that all giving be measured, for fear the fountain will run dry. As a result of this subtle distinction, the world class gives more gets more, and attracts more.

70

ACTION STEP FOR TODAY

Give money to someone who needs a few bucks, without any expectation of receiving anything in return. Maybe it's the guy begging for money on the street, or possibly a friend in need of some fast cash.

This habit manifests a prosperity consciousness that will *attract more abundance into your life.*

" I do not know how wicked American millionaires are, but as I travel about and see the results of their

generosity in the form of hospitals,

churches, public libraries, universities, parks, recreation grounds, art museums and theatres, I wonder what on earth we should do without them."

~William Lyon Phelps

The
World Class has
Great
EXPECTATIONS

One of the greatest discoveries I've made in the last two decades as a mental toughness coach is the realization that world-class performers are driven by positive expectations. In other words, the great ones always expect to win regardless of what they are up against.

The next discovery I made was that this same positive expectation could be instilled in anyone who wishes to possess it. It's a programming process that is easy to do; all it takes is desire and persistence. Champions begin this programming process by creating the language they use when they talk to themselves, as well as the pictures they visualize. World-class performers literally talk themselves into believing anything that gives them a mental edge. Call it positive brainwashing, programming, affirmation training, auto-suggestion – whatever label you choose. Champions call it their ace in the hole.

"As your consciousness expands, your level of expectation will grow. Keep asking yourself, am I selling myself short? Most of us are."

~John R. Spannuth
President, United States Water Fitness Association

While most amateur performers rely on positive experiences to build positive expectations, professional performers are superstars in their minds long before they are superstars in reality. Why wait for Mother Nature to produce snow at a ski resort when it can be artificially produced right now? Then, when it does snow, it simply adds powder to a very solid base. Expectation works whether it's built from real experience or programming. The advantage of programming is it is guaranteed to happen - while experience may or may not occur.

ACTION STEP FOR TODAY

Outline your expectations in every area of your life & then ask the ultimate CRITICAL THINKING question:

"Should I expect more?"

If your answer is yes, raise your expectations and upgrade how you talk to yourself and others about *your heightened aspirations.*

"High **achievement** always takes place
in the framework of
HIGH EXPECTATION."

~Charles Kettering

Champions are

DRIVEN

by a World-Class BELIEF SYSTEM

$\mathcal{M}$ake no mistake: champions are driven to succeed. Many believe that only some people are born with this innate aptitude of ambition. Studies show this isn't true. Champions are driven to win, in most cases, because they believe they can. If you inherited a treasure map from your best friend, would you be driven to follow the map and find the fortune? So would anyone else. If this is true, why are the majority of people simply trying to survive in a world of wealth and abundance? The answer is simple: they don't believe they can find their own treasures. This doesn't alter the fact that the treasure is there, yet it does change the drive of the performer.

The human animal is only driven to the level its belief system will allow. Most of us have been programmed by amateur performers with limited belief systems, and subsequently, small ambitions. As a result, we tend to attract other amateurs as friends, who reinforce these limited beliefs and validate our lack consciousness. This cycle spins out of control until the drive is nearly nonexistent. Amateurs rationalize their lack of drive with tall tales of bad breaks and unfortunate circumstances. Meanwhile, the champions - no more intelligent or talented - become more focused and driven every day and continue to win.

"In the second grade, they asked us **what we wanted to be.** I said I wanted to be a ball player, and they laughed. In eighth grade, they asked the same question, and I said a ball player, and they laughed a little more. By the eleventh grade, **no one was laughing.**"

~Johnny Bench
Major League Catcher

78

Action Step for Today

Generally speaking, is your belief system poverty class, middle class, or world class?

Ask this CRITICAL THINKING question:

"Do my drive and ambition mirror my beliefs?"

If you're not sure of the answer, check your results in
the areas of your life where you exhibit the most ambition.

"All the strength and force of man comes from his **faith in things unseen.** He who believes is strong; he who doubts is weak. **Strong convictions precede great actions."**

~James Freeman Clarke

Champions Take RISKS

$\mathcal{A}$verage performers are risk averse. They've been taught that to make it through life in one piece, play it safe and be thankful they have a roof over their heads. "Stay below the radar and you won't get hurt," seems to be their world view. With a mindset rooted in fear and scarcity, they unconsciously set goals of arriving safely at death.

"I don't want to find myself in a nursing home someday, thinking that all I did was play it safe."

~Charlie Eitel
Chairman/CEO
The Simmons Company

World-class performers work from an abundance-based consciousness rooted in love, which knows no limits or bounds. The pros take risks – not because they are necessarily more courageous – but because they believe they can get back anything they lose. In the minds of champions, resources and money are abundant. As a result, the fear of loss has very little influence with this group. Champions have always been risk takers, because they have come to understand that business and life are about learning and growing. How can you learn and grow when you never step out and try something new and exciting? There is never a lack of resources, only a lack of ideas. Without risk, there can be no progress. All of us only have so much sand left in the hourglass, and one day our sand will run out. The time to risk is now and the great ones know it.

ACTION STEP FOR TODAY

Learning to be comfortable when taking calculated risks is an acquired skill. The only way to develop it is to begin to take risks. Decide today to take a small risk on something you've been thinking about doing.

Feel the fear and do it anyway.

If this process is new to you, rest assured - *you will feel less fear with every risk you take.*

"Only those who will
risk going too far
can possibly find out
how far one can go."

~T. S. Eliot

SECRETS 21

the
Great Ones
Take
Responsibility

One of the critical factors separating amateurs from pros is responsibility. People operating at the poverty and working-class levels of awareness often see themselves as victims of the powerful. They create invisible mental barriers that, in their minds, hold them back from moving up. They blame other people for keeping them down, such as their parents, friends and others of influence during their childhood.

People at the middle-class level of awareness are a little more evolved, but tend to make safety and security their number one priorities. They hold on so tightly to what they have that they fail to see the real abundance staring them straight in the face. Average people in this category are terrified of losing what they have, because their mind is submerged in the cesspool of scarcity. People at this level truly believe their supply of money is limited, and if they lose what they have, they will never get it back. The majority of the population has this belief.

"Success on any major scale requires you to **accept responsibility...** In the final analysis, the one quality that **ALL** successful people have... is the ability to take on **RESPONSIBILITY.**"

~Michael Korda, Author

People operating at the upper-class level of awareness tend to be unafraid, aggressive, ultra-competitive warriors who approach life like a battle. They know there is abundance and they are out to get it. The upper class tends to operate primarily from their ego.

People at the world-class level are a step ahead of the upper class, simply because they operate from their spirit-self rather than their ego-self. The great ones have thought processes, philosophies and habits all rolled into one that overshadows the rest: I am responsible. The world class realizes it is completely responsible for its success or failure, as well as responsible for giving back some of the blessings bestowed upon it as a result of its tremendous success. Operating from a world-class level of awareness almost always precedes their success. The great ones keep marching forward, making a difference in themselves and the world.

ACTION STEP FOR TODAY

Commit to taking total responsibility for everything that happens to you. This one change in thinking has the power to launch you to the world-class level *faster than any other single idea.*

"When a man decides to do something he must go all the way, but he must take responsibility for what he does. He must know first why he is doing it and then he must proceed with his actions with no doubts or remorse."

~Carlos Castaneda

SECRETS 22

Champions
thrive on World Class
Self-Talk

$\mathcal{S}$elf-talk is what we say to ourselves all day long, and also how we say it. For years, philosophers, psychologists and performance experts worldwide have known about the impact self-talk has on us. That being said, average performers are oblivious to what they are saying to themselves and how it's affecting the quality of their lives. The pros have always been aware of the power of language in programming and reprogramming the human computer.

> ## "Repeat anything long enough & it will start to become you."
> ~Tom Hopkins
> Author, Speaker

Dr. Shad Helmstetter, in his magnificent book, *What to Say When You Talk to Yourself*, writes that up to 77% of the average person's self-talk is negative. According to Dr. Helmstetter, we spend our lives talking ourselves into and out of things. Champions believe and embrace this idea. As a matter of fact, the easiest way to know you're in the presence of champions is to listen to them. The world-class has spent years overcoming poor programming, and this process usually begins with the use of language, both with themselves and others. The great ones believe almost anything is possible, simply because they have repeated that idea – and others like it – to themselves for years. To quote Dr. Helmstetter, "Repetition is a convincing argument." Developing world-class self-talk may be the most powerful of all of the mental toughness secrets of the great ones. Like most of the habits, traits and philosophies in this book, it's so simple that it's often overlooked. As a result, amateur performers continue to perpetuate amateur language with themselves and others. Meanwhile, the great ones create ideas out of thin air, convince themselves achievement is possible, and then go out and make it happen.

ACTION STEP FOR TODAY

Begin monitoring everything you say to yourself and others.
Ask this CRITICAL THINKING question:

"Is the way I use language programming me for success or failure?"
Next, begin listening to the way people around you use language.

Ask yourself the same question about them.
This is an eye-opening experience.

"Relentless, repetitive self talk is what changes our self-image."

~Denis Waitley

SECRETS 23

the GREAT ONES make the

complicated

SIMPLE

The middle-class consciousness seems to believe that the more complicated something sounds, the more impressive it is. The world class tends to have the opposite belief. They know even the most complex ideas, philosophies or systems can be broken down into simple concepts. Albert Einstein's theory of relativity is one of the greatest discoveries of the 20th century, and even scientists agree the formula is complex. Einstein disagreed. Explaining the basic theory to a non-scientist one day he said, "Have you ever spent time with a pretty girl and the time just flew by? Have you ever spent time with someone you didn't like and the time seemed to drag on forever? That's relativity."

"Genius is the ability to reduce the complicated to the simple."

~C.W. Ceram
Roman Archeologist, Author

The great ones know true genius rests in the simplification of what appears to be complex processes. Amateurs are convinced success has to be more than the simple implementation of a few dozen key ideas, habits, thought processes and philosophies. Amateurs make the success process more complex than it is. Large corporations are made up of a series of complex systems, but every great business leader will tell you 90% of all business problems can be solved by increased sales. Champions constantly try to simplify their thoughts and ideas. Mental clarity is the cornerstone of everything they do, and simplifying things promotes greater clarity.

ACTION STEP FOR TODAY

Do a breakdown to discover the essence of what motivates, inspires and drives you, and most importantly, what makes you happy. Reduce these ideas to as few words as possible, so a fourth grader could understand what you're saying.

This exercise will elevate your level of mental clarity.

"There is a **master key to success** with which no man can fail. Its name is **SIMPLICITY,** I mean, in the sense of reducing to the simplest possible terms every problem that besets us. Whenever I have met a business proposition which, after taking thought, I could not reduce to simplicity, **I have left it ALONE."**

~Sir Henri Deterding

SECRETS 24

the
Great Ones
have a Sense of
URGENCY

*M*iddle-class performers operate like there is an endless amount of time in a day, week, month, year and life. The world class is extremely sensitive to time. The great ones have a sense of urgency because they are operating at a level of awareness that constantly reminds them the present moment is all any of us really have. The world class is on a mission to fulfill a dream, and they know the clock is ticking.

"One realizes the **full importance of time** only when there is little of it left. Every man's **greatest capital asset** is his unexpired years of **PRODUCTIVE life.**" ~P.W. Litchfield

The only time amateur performers develop a sense of urgency is toward the end of the day, week, or before they go on vacation. Imagine if they channeled that same energy, enthusiasm and focus into their everyday performances. Worldwide productivity would probably triple in one day. Professional performers constantly remind themselves that life is short and if they are going to make something happen, now is the time. This thought process makes the middle class uncomfortable. Remember, they prefer to operate in a state of mild delusion, knowing the clock is ticking and none of us know how much time we have left. This becomes too uncomfortable for emotional amateurs.

For pros, who operate from objective reality, it's a primary motivating force. It's one of the reasons the great ones tend to pursue large, magnificent visions. They know their time on earth is limited and they want to leave a legacy. Their sense of urgency goes back to the beginning of the mental toughness process – clearly defining what they want.

What do you have a sense of urgency to do? If you know the answer, you can implement this world-class philosophy immediately. If not, make it your mission to discover the embers that burn within your soul and focus that passion on what you really want. Don't stop until you find it. When you do, create a sense of urgency to act on it now. Don't hesitate. Pursue your dream boldly and fearlessly. It may be later than you think.

Action Step for Today

To heighten your sense of urgency, do a little mathematical calculation. Based on statistics, the average man living in 21st century America will live seventy-three years. The average woman will live seventy-nine years.

Based on your current age and these statistics, how many days do you have left to live?

Keep this number in front of you as a reminder the clock is ticking and there is no time to lose.

"I have been impressed with
the urgency of doing.
Knowing is not enough; we must apply.
Being willing is not enough; we must do."

~Leonardo da Vinci

the GREAT ONES are

LEARNING
Machines

For most people in modern western culture, learning means memorizing facts, theories, theorems and dates. That's what most of us were taught to do in school. To average people, learning is a late-night cram session and a pot of coffee to stay awake.

Professional performers have overcome this outdated, industrial-age system and created a formula for learning and developing their minds. As speaker Jim Rohn says, "Formal education will make you a living; self-education will make you a fortune." The pros know this to be accurate, and invest heavily in books, tapes and CD programs on everything from personal development to sales, marketing and management. They read and study trade journals and become world-renowned experts. Average people spend less than ten dollars annually on books. The top 1% of income earners in America invests nearly $10,000 annually on books and other learning resources. They attend seminars, workshops and retreats.

"An organization's **ability to learn,** and translate that learning into action rapidly, is the ultimate competitive **business advantage.**"

~ Jack Welch
Former Chairman and CEO
General Electric

Amateur performers look at these investments as a waste of time and money. They are more likely to invest their money in lottery tickets, satellite television, cigarettes, alcohol and other forms of entertainment. The great ones, in the words of scientific genius Buckminster Fuller, "Dare to be naïve." The middle class thinks they have little left to learn. World-class performers know the more they learn, the greater the level of awareness they reach; and the greater the level of awareness, the more they realize how much more there is left to learn. The great ones know learning, like love, is infinite. There is no end until their hearts stop beating.

Action Step for Today

Make a commitment to develop your own self-education program.
Read, listen and attend seminars and workshops. Set a goal to read a certain
number of books and listen to a set number of CDs each month.

This shift in lifestyle will catapult your career
and your consciousness.

"As long as you live,
**keep learning how to
live."**

~Lucius Annaeus Seneca

SECRETS 26

the Great Ones Use Mentors

The masses are content to acquire knowledge, information and wisdom the old-fashioned way – from experience. Champions are different. They believe in working smarter, not harder. This means learning from mentors and coaches, who have the ability to accelerate the process exponentially. My late friend and client, Walter Hailey, the famous entrepreneur from Texas, used to say the secret to his success was his ability to "copy genius."

Instead of investing years in the school of hard knocks, the world class often reaches their heights by standing on the shoulders of giants. Champions are famous for building mentor teams who are already where they want to be.

"The ultimate source of **information,** and the whole world's living wisdom, lies in the MINDS OF OTHERS...

ALL YOU HAVE TO DO IS

ASK."

~Walter Hailey, 1928-2003, Entrepreneur, Speaker

Corporations call this group a board of directors. Individuals call it a mentor team. Mentor teams guide, teach, advise and encourage performers to think bigger and reach higher than ever before. They often provide specialized knowledge and contacts linked to the area of life in which the performer needs assistance. The overall task of mentors is to help performers raise their levels of awareness and expectation. Mentors are continually prodding and pushing champions beyond their comfort zones. The major advantage of the mentor team is the speed with which it accelerates the performer's growth. While average people expand their consciousness at a steady rate, the mentor team demands rocket-like acceleration from its charges. The mentor team is an ace in the hole for champions.

ACTION STEP FOR TODAY

Make a list of the five most successful people you know and make a commitment to use the *"copy genius' philosophy"* with them.

"It requires wisdom to **understand wisdom:**
the **music is NOTHING** if the
audience is **deaf."**

~Walter Lippmann

STEVE SIEBOLD

*S*teve Siebold, CSP, CPCS, is an internationally recognized expert in the field of mental toughness training. His Fortune 500 clients include Johnson & Johnson™, Procter & Gamble™, GlaxoSmithKline™, Toyota™ and Harrah's Entertainment™. His first book, *177 Mental Toughness Secrets of the World Class*, sold over 100,000 copies.

As a professional speaker, Steve addresses approximately 60 live audiences per year and ranks among the top 1% of income earners worldwide. In 2007, Steve won the prestigious Telly Award for most outstanding host for his national television show, Mental Toughness of Champions. In 2009, he co-starred in the feature film, *Beyond the Secret*, the long awaited follow up to the mega-hit movie, *The Secret*, which was seen by over 1 billion people worldwide. Steve resides in Palm Beach County, Florida and Lake Lanier, Georgia, with wife Dawn and family animals Robin the rat dog and sugar gliders Einstein and Maslow.

To learn more about Steve Siebold visit www.govesiebold.com. Steve can be reached at 1-877-789-2915 or asksteve@govesiebold.com

The
simple truths®
DIFFERENCE

If you have enjoyed this book we invite you to check out our entire collection of gift books, with free inspirational movies, at **www.simpletruths.com.**

You'll discover it's a great way to inspire friends and family, or to thank your best customers and employees.

We would love to hear how Simple Truths books enrich your life and others around you. Please send your comments to:

Simple Truths Feedback
1952 McDowell Road, Suite 300
Naperville, IL 60563

Or e-mails us at: comments@simpletruths.com

Or call us toll free:
800-900-3427